LIVING IN THE FORTIES

Edited By

TRUDI PURDY

First published in Great Britain in 1993 by
ARRIVAL PRESS
3 Wulfric Square, Bretton,
Peterborough, PE3 8RF

Foreword

Living in the Forties is a bittersweet anthology
of memories from people who remember the
Forties. Ranging from poems about Spam to
blackouts; rationing to the Black Market; chew-
ing gum to dried eggs! Looking back at life with
both seriousness and humour.

If you remember the Forties then you will be
able to identify with the poems that fill this
book. For those of you who do not remember,
this is a collection that will give you a feel for
how people lived during a decade, half of which
was war torn. Poignant memories of courage and
camaraderie are penned with depth and feeling.
Would it be safe to say that everyone looks back
at parts of their lives and remembers them as *the
good ole days*?

I think that this book will be enjoyed by both
young and old alike. I know I enjoyed compiling
it and hope that you get as much insight from
Living in the Forties as I did.

Trudi Purdy

Contents

But Not Forgotten

The war behind us, peace came slowly.
Victory bonfires, figures dancing
dark against their light, recalled
the lurid skies of war-torn London,
helmeted figures grimly hauling
the dead and dying from the heaps
of rubble that had once been streets.

At home we tried to avoid going past
the burned-out farm next door, its stench
the smell of our remembered fear,
the Clydeside blitz, when bombers left
buildings sliced open, flats like shelves
spilling out bed-clothes, carpets, mixed
with yellow dust of shattered walls.

But peace-time still meant ration books,
the wartime loaf, corned beef, dried egg,
gas masks still hanging in the hall.
Nylons were rare; we counted coupons
for each new blouse, each pair of shoes,
until normality flowed back
with even bananas in the shops.

So peace came slowly, but some things
are slow to die, past tense but not
forgotten. Even now I hate to close
shutters at night, and five o'clock
sees every light switched on, and dread
of passing ambulances' sirens
or drone of night planes overhead.

Dorothy Whamond

1

Spam

The nicest thing that we enjoyed
In 'forty-two, was spam.
'Twas introduced to take the place
Of non-existant ham.
All else we ate was packed and sealed
In portions very small;
When served, they'd whet the appetite
And that was about all.
Butter, sugar, fats and cheese,
Were rationed, as were meats;
And coupons had to be produced
For clothes and precious sweets:
But we survived, not just because
Of Churchill's words so bold,
Or yet because the few's first flights
Put Hitler's planes on hold,
But when an ally overseas,
Well-known as Uncle Sam,
Sent over, with the armaments,
Ten thousand tons of spam.

Margaret Smith

Wartime Farewell

At the station, by the train.
A close embrace, a lingering kiss.
Wondering when we'll meet again
And repeat this fleeting moment's bliss.

Last farewells are hastily said.
The train moves off and gathers speed.
No one knows what lies ahead,
But fate already, has been decreed.

J P R Vernon

Forties Wedding

February forty seven
Was the month and year we wed.
Food and clothing still on ration,
But we were quite well fed.

Borrowed gown and borrowed veil
Fruit for the cake was found,
Home made wine for the toast,
And smiling faces all around.

Deep snow lay round about.
Starting early in November
Staying with us many months.
Quite cold as I remember.

As I walked along the church footpath,
Snow crept through each silver shoe.
While the photographs were taken,
Bride and bridesmaid were turning blue.

All that was many years ago,
But memories come flooding back.
As I look out of my window,
And see the pure white snow.

Cicely Heathers

The Home Front in the 40's

Reserved Occupation. A doddle? Not quite.
Full stretch at the factory; fire-watching at night,
With fire-fighting training for housewives still free;
On look-out for lights which an airman might see.
With any time over - the Services Club.
Most Sundays - the Red Cross, collecting the blood,
Or Digging for Victory, growing some food
To eke out the rations for us and our brood.
If good fortune favoured, we'd buy us some fags,
Or baccy to make them. Put on our glad rags
And go to the pictures; there, out of the light
Indulge in a snooze, making up for a night
On ARP watch, with the 'planes overhead;
Ack-ack from the park to stop bombs being shed.
We're glad that the kids in the country are safe,
Though the War Office 'gram takes the smile from our face.

All that, and much more, till they dropped that small bomb;
Then one slightly bigger. They said we had won.

Street Victory Parties.
                    The bill to be paid.
We'll have a new Government most of us said
We'll put into practice the Beveridge Report,
Have fair shares for all. Well at least that's the thought.

But whether it works or whether it doesn't
I'll leave you to guess. For me - well I wouldn't.

Tom Gibbons

Living in the 40's

The air-raid sirens wailed - the German bombers neared,
A daylight raid on London then our fighter planes appeared
Swooping, diving, wheeling, a bomber seen to stall,
We left our work when ordered to, as bombs began to fall,
Took shelter in the basement, but idleness soon palls,
No damage done to Bond Street, but very near St Pauls.

Night - distant blood-red sky - was easy to discern,
From our home in North West London, we watched the
                                              East End burn.
The courage of those firemen deserve the highest praise,
The spirit of the people helped them through those awful days.
A friend, wed in Stepney, small reception complete,
Despite rationing, in the one house left in that ruined street.

Call-up papers came, sad to leave both home and work,
But arms were badly needed after losses at Dunkirk,
Sent to the Midlands - to the quiet countryside,
Girls came from every corner of the British Isles with pride,
Working like demons, to slacken was a crime,
Our orders were completed in a record-breaking time.

The bells rang out - what joy - when victory was won,
The sacrifice, the courage of the gallant allies sung,
Farewell friends, home again - to work I found nearby,
More confident, whereas before, so desperately shy.
Theatres, holidays, sport again to treasure,
But horrors of the holocaust - we can never measure.

A Le Petit

6

Spon Street

If you ever visited Spon Street,
In the city of Coventry,
When the shop doors stood wide open,
You were treated with civility.

Whether bread or meat or a little treat
These shops would all provide,
They were not very big, no *SUPERSTORES*,
But a welcome you would find inside.

There were Don and Pam at the Butcher's shop,
No room for *trolleys* there,
But the best of meat and a welcome seat,
While served with the utmost care.

Oh what a joy to stand and chat,
As you waited your pork to be chined,
Or maybe you fancied a pie or some ham
Home cooked, the best you could find.

There was Robin at the Baker's
With Dad and Philip too,
Who arrived before St John's struck four,
Their wholesome task to do.

Oh the smell of the bread all made by hand,
Was the finest you could buy,
Large ones, small ones, buns and cakes,
And on Fridays, a real apple pie.

But alas, alas, in Spon Street, a change has taken place,
No little shops like there used to be,
No cobbled street or gaiters to the knee,
But one big race to find a place in the *car park*.
M L Daly

Christmas 1943

A cuddly boy,
A poor fir tree,
With cotton balls
Amongst the green.
A precious egg
For Christmas fare,
Daddy somewhere *over there*.
Once more the magic seemed to be,
Yet no bells rang
To set us free.
The Christmas message
Seemed important, then -
Joy, and peace.
Goodwill towards men.

M Marfurt

8

Not Tonight Adolf Please

Is that the air raid siren,
my word, old Jerry's early tonight.
for God's sake draw the curtains,
we musn't show a light.

Let's all go down to the cellar,
light the candles, follow me.
It's really no good worrying,
for what's to be will be.

But when the bombs come hurtling down
you can only hold your breath and pray.
And hope your luck stays with you
just to live another day.

Bang, bang, bang, here they come again,
It sounds like the end of the street.
Whistles blowing and fire bells clanging
and the tramp of running feet.

It's the small house on the corner,
Mrs Thomas lived there with her cat.
But now it's only dust and rubble
and absolutely flat.

Day after day, night after night,
it's enough to make strong men weep.
I think I'll write to Mr Hitler.
Please take an evening off, and let's catch up with our sleep.

D T Wicking

The Queue

'They've got Apples up at Smith's and Tomatoes
Selling them at two o'clock,' said my neighbour
Another Queue! That is how my days are spent
Still - Apples - *and* Tomatoes! So I went
Decided to take my eldest, make her useful, might as well
the impending embarrassment I could not foretell
the Ration per customer was but a pound
For a family it would scarce go round
I drilled her well before we went
'You're not with me - ' I said with look intent
'You take your place in the queue
You're not with me, I'm not with you.'
The queue was long the day was hot
Bored, with aching feet, that was our wartime lot
As my daughter reached her goal
The heat must have taken toll
She turned, and called - Boy was I rattled!
'Mom was it a pound of tomatoes or Apples?'
Smirks and titters all around
I felt like sinking in the ground
I nodded - *'Both!'* I gruffly said
Feeling foolish with face bright red

Mary Jones

Poppy Fields

Behold humanity distraught with fears
Lost in a whirlpool of futile tears -
Stench of the slumlands, hiding of truth
Weary of waiting unredeemed youth.

Saw a vast army dripping with gore
Blindly ignoring wars gone before.
Heard the wild flying shrapnel in flight
Trailing a havoc of pitying sight.

Friendship is waning freedom is lost
Peace on a billow of doom is tossed.
Useless this building strongholds of hate
Soon will the others retaliate.

What of the ideals - progress of years!
Where is the faith and trust that endears?
Let us take heed of humanity's call
Sharing together friendship of all.

Munition work was ending, in nineteen forty five
But soldiers on the battle field who lost in the attack
Are sleeping in the poppy fields and never coming
back!

Wesley Price

1941

Against Mother's wishes Father put
a billiard table in the drawing room.
At night when sirens sounded we went
downstairs and huddled underneath it,
parents one end, Eileen the Irish maid and I
the other. When a bomb did fall

close, it wasn't the metallic crash
you hear on films, more a petulant slapping
sound, like wet cloth on stone,
and then a breath as if a giant passed
running his fingers over tiles and chimneys
to bring them spattering down. I heard a shaky

'All right darling?' from my Mother, then
like black dust the night would settle down
and we would doze till the All Clear, though
perhaps Eileen, so close now to my Father,
would reach back in the dark, soft as a moth,
and touch his hair.

Eleanor Maxted

12

A Child's Fear

We oft' heard boots go stomping
Along our country lane,
Strange dialects were talking,
The language though, the same.

We saw they had erected
A British army camp,
Where soldiers, all selected,
Marched often, wet and damp.

Our village life proceeded,
We children unaware
Which regiments resided,
Or who was stationed there.

But knew they all had flat tin hats,
And sergeants wore three stripes,
Eighth army men were *Desert Rats*
And KOYLI's *Yorkshire Tykes.*

One day, I saw a helmet strange
Upon a soldier's head,
and fear so did my brain derange
That from *the foe* I fled.

I knew the helmet shape was wrong,
His gaiters, quite wrong too,
And no way did those boots belong,
Soft soles, ours never knew.

When breathless, but inside our door
My fears came loud and shrill,
One sister shrieked, *there may be more,*
My heart sank lower still.

But Father, who I felt, would know,
Said, 'Pray girl, calm you fear,
We needed help to fight the war.
The Americans are here.'

Grace Leeder-Jackson

14

So Young to Live: So Old to Die

At seventeen I went to war
My Uncle Jim, he'd been before
His tales they were so full of woe
I thought of them at Scapa Flow
My ship set forth for Reykjavik
The mighty seas made strong men sick
And then alarm bells began to go
Just when the wind started to blow
Old Chalky then he's heard to shout
For Pete's sake turn this ship about
A kind old lad, always a grin
Too bad the sea 'twas done him in
A wave then crashed upon the deck
He cried 'Oh, what the 'eck,'
But suddenly he vanished overboard
No sound, no sigh, not e'en a word
We screamed and shouted through the night
'Chalky, Chalky, you all right?'
Alas, he vanished in the deep
I thought about it in my sleep
And vowed that I would always know
That Chalky died so long ago
Within the sight of Reykjavik.
To some he seemed just a name
To add to war's long list of shame
For me old Chalky will remain
My dear old friend, beyond life's pain
and now old pal I think of you
Fond memories, so real, so true.

Cyril Saunders

15

Loud Nights

They were the brave days, the forties, I remember,
Anything was possible as hours would expand
To include all you wanted to do.
The time to rest was when the sky was invaded
By the thundering hordes of enemy wings.
The time to awaken was the start of a new day
To a quietened dawn of dust and destruction.
And if you were on your feet helping with salvation
You knew you'd survived another loud night.
Hurry to get your bus on the road
Helping people to take up their work load.
The day would progress with a semblance of norm,
And people with a modicum of time would stand
Queueing for nylons or anything to hand,
Until the dusk and the wail of sirens
Heralded the thundering night time again.

Edna Tunstead

The Vacant Chair

They gather round the fireside in the twilight of the year:
Recapturing all those happy times - a son so loved and dear:
So oft they pause to glimpse again, that ever vacant chair -
The humble family dwelling - with its memories everywhere.

The favourite pictures still on wall - same furniture arranged,
Chintz covers old and faded - the casement scene unchanged:
But now no laughter fills the air - no voice in harmony:
A hush has so descended - and all so suddenly:

From babyhood they'd watched him grow - the future seemed assured.
No thought of dimming glory, till to battle he was lured. . .
Then the hill was steep and rugged, sunlight erased from view:
Tranquillity had been disturbed. But a prayer for hope anew.

The cruel blow it left behind a wild destructive sting:
The flame of courage flickered - farewell to everything. . .
A victim of the conflict, he had paid the supreme price -
For loved ones round the fireside - for mankind - the sacrifice.

Joan Higgins

I Remember

In the forties there were many lonely brides,
The bombs were falling and more besides.
The children left their homes, eyes full of tears,
To keep them safe and live devoid of fears.
Our hearts went out to parents left behind,
Who slaved at any job, that they could find.

Pull in your belts and dig the ground,
Dig for Victory was the common sound.
Be like the bees, fill up your hives
And remember *careless talk costs lives*
The atom bomb; then all was over
Our ships returned with men to Dover.

In forty five, church bells rang out,
'Twas Peace on Earth, the merry shout.
Our children now are coming home
Back to the streets they'd always known,
Such happiness with dirty faces
Brought love to the old familiar places.

Vera Hansson

A Child's War

The evacuee's came, with their
Pale city faces.
From bomb blitzed London
Clutching gas respirators
Folk welcomed and made them
All feel at ease;
The school classes extended.
It became quite a squeeze!

Billeted soldiers
Changing village life so. . .
That quite often the
Challenge would come
Friend or foe?

Duties of Home Guard
Not all sweetness and light;
You're required at the post.
Came the call, late at night!

Black out for the windows -
Not a light must be shown
Ears strained through the silence
Catch the spitfires low drone.

From airfields in East Anglia
With mission in sight,
God willing, returning - by dawn's early light.

Utility clothes and rationing of meat
Powdered eggs -
Oh, and coupons for sweets!
American GI's and *Got any gum?*
Candy and nylons
Plus jitterbug fun.

Vera Lynn (forces' sweetheart)
Winston Churchill our pride
We prayed *God be with us*
Our nation to guide.

Through the eyes of a child
This was all that I saw.
Of a heart rending conflict;
The Second World War.

Brenda L Hudson

Per Ardua Ad Astra

Maybe
   somewhere up there,
      a new distant star
         shines bright.

For
   I bade farewell
      to my chum,
         as they hosed out
            his turret
               last night.

Ilston Charles Butlin

War

How awful are the spoils
of war
The crashing bomb
The dog fight o'er
We hear not
The cries
Of anguished men
Whose loved ones
Even now
Write with fevered pen
Still they wait
For news
Or letters through
The door
Not knowing all is lost
There will be
No more

S May

From My Flying Log-Book

On a day in April '41
this erk was so uptight
when climbing up in a Dominie
for his very first flight.

On the tenth of July '41
a Whitley took the air
for an air-sea firing exercise
I know 'cos I was there.

Then in to September '41
I joined an OT U
for more training on a Wellington
and so I joined a crew.

On to the thirteenth of December
from Portreath we did go
took eleven hours to Gibralter
today you'd think *that's slow!*

To Egypt and Squadron 38
for some bombing action
mine-laying the harbour - Banghazi
was the prime attraction.

On July twenty-third '42
on final *Op* of tour
with heavy ack-ack over Tobruk
I did not yearn for more.

A second tour with the Pathfinders
in 1945
in Lancasters over Germany
Then glad to be alive.
Cyril Harding

The Tenements

Tenements in the forties, were not so bad
when I played there as a lad.
Memories of the ritual for the big and small
collecting a ha'penny for a tanner ball.
For this to us was a nightly treat,
playing football on the street.
Six goals to be scored afore half-time
an' thirteen to cross the winning line.
When football we could play no more
we played with the lasses at the doors.
Up and down the stairs we ran
playing *I spy* and *Kick the can.*
Doctors and nurses was another game
where bold lads could find some fame
by being banished in disgrace,
for being wounded in a naughty place.
Having to take the good with the bad
some days got you, oh so mad.
With one lavvy on each stair-head
can you imagine the palaver, when in need.
Racing to the one above, or the one below
an' finding the queue just as slow.
With toilet paper on the ration
The daily newspaper was the fashion.
Thursday night was also, one of dread,
The weekly bath, afore going to bed.
with the zinc-tub on the floor
you were scrubbed until you were sore.
Oh, happy days, in the tenements.

W Carmichael

24

V J Day

Many years have now gone by
Since war, so far away did cease,
And we in England breathed a prayer
That we might have a lasting peace.

And memories come back to me
Of days, now long since gone,
Wondering what was happening
In the land of the rising sun.

Pearl Harbour started the conflict;
How swiftly the Japs overran
Manila, New Guinea and Java -
All fell to the Nipponese van.

The infamous Burma railroad,
And women and children immured
In cruel prisoner-of-war camps,
Privation and tortures endured.

But the end came very swiftly
When their cities were destroyed
By the atom bombs that were dropped,
leaving a devastated void.

And so today I say a prayer -
May all the battle flags stay furled,
May atom bombs be ever banned,
And peace reign over all the world.

Milly Blane

Memories of 1940 World War Two

Working in a factory on war work
helping to fight the foe,
But what all the fighting was about
I was too young to know.

Blacked out were the streets
you could not see a thing, yet
in every factory you would hear
the girls all sing.

A time we helped each other
through those dark dismal days
How our parents coped with it all
they all deserve our praise.

Rationing with Ration Books
we all got the same
Coupon Books for buying clothes
Utility was the name

Oh memories come flooding back some happy
yet some sad.
But I must say thank you once again
to my lovely Mum and Dad.

I Platt

Forty Four

I sailed the sea in an LST*
my God, how she did roll,
up came breakfast, dinner and tea
and I all but lost my soul.

I did a spell in Chatham Town
Life was bad, and a misery,
The bloody barracks got me down
I'd much rather be back at sea.

All in all I enjoyed my time
and I would do it all again,
in peace it would be mighty fine
a holiday at three score and ten.

*Landing Ship Tank

Charles Boor

The Voice

And now the voice that fell on heedless ears
   Is listened to at last: a clarion call
Rousing the nation from its doubts and fears;
   Inspired; inspiring; offering each and all
Nothing but blood and toil and sweat and tears;
   But offering *victory* - though the heavens fall.

And Britain, offering *him* commanding power,
Has found the man to match her finest hour.

T V Newmark

Wartime Days

In the nineteen forties when England was at war
I lived in a country cottage and draughts blew through the door
Quiet evenings by the fire, papers in the rack,
Although my feet were nice and warm, I shivered at the back.

No standard lamp to read by, no chandelier array,
But an old, old lamp, with blackened glass which I filled with oil each day.
I didn't own a TV set or a telephone in the hall
No fridge to keep the butter cool just a meat-safe on the wall

In the nineteen forties when times were very hard
No water from an indoor tap, just an old pump in the yard
I didn't own a motor car, no bus passed by my door
No supermarket *help yourself* just a friendly village store.

I hadn't got a Barclay Card, or a meter with a slot
No package holidays abroad spending cash I hadn't got,
No sirloin joint, or leg of lamb, or rare rump steak to fry,
My rations wouldn't stand to that, so I lived on rabbit pie.

There were gas masks and ration books, and planes droned over head,
And blackout curtains closely drawn, when, each night I went to bed
With all the comforts of today, my share, I must admit
But, to go back to those war time days I wouldn't mind one bit!

Elizabeth Davey

I Remember

The siren's eerie wailing
as the War-planes flew apace.
Concern for Friends and Relatives.
Adopting a *Brave Face*.

Smoky, Crowded Caverns
under Railway termini.
Aircraft droning overhead.
Searchlights in the sky.

Sisalcraft on wooden frames
to black out window panes.
Stepping over sleeping soldiers
in the corridors of trains.

Airplanes, swooping, Diving.
Vapour trails on high.
The crackle of machine guns.
Dog-fights in the Sky.

Standing on a Kentish Hill.
East London all aflame.
September 7th, 1940.
The Day the Bombers came!

Ration Books and I D Cards
Petrol Coupons too.
The vanishing of *Them* and *Us*.
The change to *Me* and *You*.

How, in sharing Danger
we learned to care a lot.
But I most of all, remember
how quickly we forgot!

Harold King

The Fight for Tomorrow

My mind drifts back to those dark days
when war took its heavy toll.
To each came the parting of the ways,
to reach a common goal.

Ration books for food and clothes
ensure fair shares for all.
Evacuees move out in droves,
where safer pastures call.

Frightened little faces peer
from windows of the train.
Mothers try to hide their fear.
Will they see their child again?

Blackout curtains, no lights about.
When Air Raid Wardens see a glow
they call, 'Put that light out,
there's a war on don't you know!'

The year was nineteen forty four.
Came a new and ominous sound.
The V1 zoomed in with a roar,
then silent, it fell to the ground.

The doodlebugs, as they were named,
did at random fall.
Many were the people maimed,
loved ones beyond recall.

Through the pain and sorrow,
the spirit did not wane.
But fought for that tomorrow
when the lights went on again.
G E Fitzgerald

Glimpses of the Early Forties

The sky lit up with flames
Exciting for child to see.
Barrage-balloons exploded!
We screamed aloud with glee!
One fell down in Gran's garden
Shocked Gran much more than me.

Awakened in the night
Wrapped snug in eiderdown.
Carried to next door's shelter
That was below the ground.
My Grandad on night duty
As shrapnel fell around.

Saw Pompey the next morning
Reduced to smoking stones
People salvaging special things
'Twas all that's left of home.
Trying to put a brave face on
No-one sat around or moaned.

Waiting for Dad to come back home
With buttons shining bright.
Stranger to wartime children
His leaves would us excite.
Meeting his ship in S'hampton
Was such an awesome sight!

Bananas, oranges were new things
We had to learn about.
Sweets in cone twisted packets
Weekly rations were eked out.
Parcels came from Dad abroad
These carefully were shared out.
Pat Rees

The Birds Still Sang

The sirens wailed as enemy planes flew overhead,
Flares, sallied earthwards, turning silver sky to red,
Showers of incendiaries scattered everywhere,
Whistles as the screaming bombs came plunging through the air;
Swish, then boom, the tinkling sound of glass,
A moment's respite followed by another awful crash:
Shelters full of people trying to be brave,
Wardens giving comfort, trying lives to save:-

After the *All Clear* had died, I strolled along
The bomb scarred streets, my duty done,
When suddenly, my heart relieved of momentary pang,
Felt a heartening surge of joy - because the birds still sang -
Yes, sang, their early morning voices still
Rang out, a sweet and never ending trill.
I stood exalted! For from terror, crash and bang,
They gave their ray of comfort, those birds still sang.

Henrietta Ross Hodgson

Siren

The wail of the siren screamed and whined,
Hurrying footsteps, scurrying feet,
The nurses' stiff skirts rustling
As their busy hands folded the sheet.

They lifted him onto the trolley,
Squeaking wheels, rumbling floor,
And as they pushed they heard the growl
Of the pulsing engines' roar.

Turning and twisting, long corridors,
Jolting and jerking - stars of pain -
And the earth exploding, the walls crumbling,
With plaster and dusty rain.

The trolley jacked upwards against the door,
He ground his teeth - helpless lay -
The nurses shook the dirt from their hair
And took him through the bay.

They reached the hospital's shelter,
A crack - a bursting shell -
And calls and shouts of the crowded room
As the ceiling tilted and fell.

A sudden break - a silence -
He held his breath, his cry,
A nurse's hand crept into his,
A warmth - a comfort - a sigh -

Esme Francis

Grandpa Remembers

D'you remember the war, Gramp, remember it still?
Yes I remember, guess I always will
In fact it is something I'd rather forget
But in quiet moments, I think of it yet

In the Battle of Britain, the pilot and crew,
Were only young fellows, not much older than you
When the call came to *Scramble* they were never quite sure
If they'd be one of the *few* whose luck would endure

And when on the beaches, our troops were in trouble
All the small boats went to help, at the double
And that's why, so often, you'll hear people say
We could do with the Dunkirk Spirit today

There were those whose ways were not so endearing
The Spivs who made profit from black-marketing
no motive but greed - no sense of occasion
For those who risked death in D Day invasion

There were girls who'd go out with Yankee GIs
Gifts of chocolate and nylons brought stars to their eyes
The poor British soldier just couldn't compete
When a guy from the States swept his girl off her feet

There were times when we Brits had our backs to the wall
And no-one gave much for our chances at all
But we were a people who had to be free
From someone as evil as Hitler could be

So I went to the war and I did what I could
It wasn't all bad but it sure wasn't good
Sometimes we've no choice, we must fight for a cause
But I pray you won't learn for yourself, about wars.
Margaret Myttion

Palindrome

I remember now the cornfields in the Isle where I was born,
where the poppies and cornflowers her lovely lanes adorn.
I remember how the morning milk gleamed yellow in the dawn
and the sun would shine forever, in the place where I was born.

The milk was gently ladled in a measure from the churn,
where the cart stopped at the corner by the barn.
I would go there with my sisters, and was told that I must learn;
that as soon as I was big I'd take my turn.

Fetching water was much further, from the well in Market Street,
but we didn't think it strange to use our feet.
We learned the proper value of good water, fresh and sweet,
as we carried it with care from Market Street.

Uncle Augie in the High Street boiled the sweets and baked the bread,
and perhaps that's why I thought that he was God.
He'd a monstrous white-clad belly on a level with my head
and he gave us all, in turn, our daily bread.

I remember now with gratitude the country-rich warm smell
of the dung-cart and its driver, who would tell
the age-old tales of fairies in the depths of Dingle Dell,
lending magic to the words I knew so well.

They talk of second childhood in a man who's grown mature
and learned that there is nothing quite so sure
as the knowledge that the life of man will never be more pure
than the simple things of childhood that, in spite of all, endure.

Bill Shorto

First Kiss

The bombs rained down
She fled her town
Only fourteen with a Brummie twang
She joined our little gang

At sweet sixteen loved by us all
Make your choice, came the call
She stood in silence aside
Then turned to me wide eyed
'I want you,' she sighed

My heart stood still
I was amazed
Weediest of the bunch but stayed
And then she kissed me

War ended
Peace descended
Home she returned
I was not spurned
We still met but not so often
But then one day a lie was spoken
The bond was broken

Time passed by, we went our ways
I chose another
But in all those days
I thought of her
Sparkling eyes gleaming
I'm still dreaming, of that
First Kiss

Roy Whitfield

V E Night
(Victory in Europe, May 8th 1945)

Turn on the lights,
let street lamps burn away the dark
and, stark reminder, *Bombers' Moon*,
that pale conspirator,
serve sentence in a weary world -
shine Hope. Walk free
the shuttered, blacked-out
souls of night - discard *Utility*,
the Cinderella drab - and dance
with Princely strangers in the streets
before a slippered dawn
makes pumpkins out of dreams.
Dance round the bonfires of our youth,
plant poppies in the gaping wounds
and, from the rubbish heaps of war,
rise up, rejoice with rusty bells
(long silent sentinels) - give voice.
And then...go home, go softly home,
to think upon a crooked cross
and mend a crooked door.

Josie Davies

Wartime

A call up letter came
To report to the *ATS*
I caught a Leicester train
And met up with the rest.

We lined up for our uniform
A varied, motley crew
A different world had opened up
For the likes of me and you

We learnt to march in step
Across the Barracks Square
A sergeant shouting out
'Pick those knees up there.'

The Chief of General Staff
Told us secrets we must keep
About the Army Manoeuvres
And then rode off in his Jeep

The sky was full of aeroplanes
Crossing overseas
The noise of gunfire could be heard
Carried on the breeze

When the War was over
We went our separate ways
But the friendships made in the Army
We knew would always stay

A F Shaxted

Fears of the 40's

I wonder are you old enough, to recall the wartime years
When normal folk like you and I, lived with constant fears?
Not the fear of suffering, or losing their own lives.
Their fears were for their sons and daughters, husbands and their wives.
It was family friends and freedom, that they feared to lose the most.
To say they'd little fear of death, would be no idle boast
Facing death took courage, facing life for some, took more.
I lived and worked and served with them, all through the second war.
Many saw their homes destroyed, and loved ones in their graves,
Which just served to strengthen their resolve, never to be slaves.
I pray, that never more to Western Europe, will the curse of war return,
As it has in Eastern Countries, where death reigns, and houses burn.
If only we could find the Spirit, we knew in time of war,
And then combine our efforts, to cure that running sore.

Ray Baker

Memories of the Forties

Life in the forties meant war for me,
Of sorrow and partings from one's family
Of nights spent in dug-outs and damp air
Of shelves in the pantry almost bare.
The sirens shrilling in our ears,
Giving us warning and filling us with fear,
The sounds of the bombers high overhead,
Few of us ever got to bed.
Guns resounding, seeming quite near,
Noisy to our ears, and smoking the air.
Dear God! We pray night and day
Please when will it all go away.
And we can be at peace again,
With no more worry, no more pain.

Eleanor Friston

41

Living in the Forties

I met and married a long time ago
Had to work long hours and wages were low
No TV just a wireless, times sure were hard
Just a tap in the sink, or a walk down the yard,
No holidays abroad, lino on the floor
But people were friendly, no need to lock doors.

It was safe to go out for a walk in the park,
No need to stay indoors when it got dark.
No scandals, no muggings, there was nothing to rob.
And you really felt rich if you had a few bob.

People were happy in those far off days
Kinder and caring in so many ways.
But now I'm alone, and look back through the years
I remember the blessings I remember the love,
And for all of these things I thank
The Good Lord above.

Grace Clarke

War 1942

Bombs now hurtle on the Town
The streets alight and bare,
Bang bang banging in the Clouds,
Gun fire everywhere.

Shelters full, guards race around,
Frozen feet are stamped on ground.
Mothers hug their babies tight
Children sit and cry with fright.

How many hours can one hour be
When face to face with Eternity?
This War of hate, and lust, and fear,
Oh will it last another year?

And will we all grow old and bent
From lack of sleep and nourishment?
How is it bad men keep their life
When millions die in pain and strife?

At last the Sirens shrieking call
Go home, and hope the house stands tall.

Margaret Swann

Living in the Forties

The war years were not easy
With rationing with us then,
Clothes and food were rather scarce,
Sweets too, for the children.

With such a little piece of meat,
We must make a stew
With vegetables, suet dumplings,
Home-grown potatoes, too.

So we made do and mend,
Managed with what we had.
Of course we wished the war would end,
For war is very bad.

Still, all in all, we got along
Until the cease-fire came.
Soon things were back to normal,
Though never quite the same.

Doris Prowse

Window Shopping Christmas 1949

How much is that dolly in the window?
The one in the pretty pink dress.
I do love that doll in the window,
the one with the golden tress.
There are Ludos and Draughts and books galore
and wind-up trains that run round the floor.
There are smart tin soldiers in blue and red suits
and a brown teddy bear in bright yellow boots.
There's a big shiny ball with stripes red and green
and a pencil box fit for a queen.
That beautiful doll to me would be heaven
but the price on the box says *two and eleven*.
I know that money is very short,
there's bread and cheese and *marge* to be bought
and the lovely doll with her curls hanging free
is for some little girl - but it won't be me.

Eileen Rippon

Evacuées

Taken from home towns,
  From families torn,
Put into billets,
  Bewildered, forlorn,
Children missed mothers,
  They shed bitter tears,
Hit by the hardship
  Of those dreary years.
Hating the blackout,
  They dreamed of bright lights,
For nothing cheered up
  Their dark winter nights.

Time passed in home towns,
  Then appeared traces
Of happy children
  With smiling faces.
Restored to loved ones,
  Loneliness banished,
Exiles no longer,
  Every fear vanished,
United families
  At last were at peace,
No more sad partings,
  No evacuées.

Doris E Briggs

Awake to Horror

The whine of *the bombers*,
Day and night, night and day,
A prayer, in haste,
To the shelter, out we fly,

The guns in the street,
Brave men, no fear,
Fighting for liberty,
A new beginning,

Children searching for shrapnel,
Exchanging for a piece of chocolate,
Flour bags, for curtains
Dyed a pretty blue,

We are British all through
No one, tells us what to do,
Our brave, young and old,
Never to be forgotten.

Florence E Roberts

A Quiet Night

All is quiet and very still,
as the moon comes up o'er yonder hill.

The stars shine bright from a velvet sky,
could peace be near, I wonder with a sigh.

Some nights the sky is filled with darkness,
no moon, no stars, just gloom and blackness.

When the droning sound of planes are heard,
and sirens shatter the stillness of our world.

We run to shelters in the ground,
like rabbits, when the farmer is around.

But it's not the farmer we fear with his gun,
it's the bombs of our enemy, we call the Hun.

They come in the night to destroy our land,
our houses and buildings topple, like castles in the sand.

Soon, very soon, we hope that peace will come,
a peace that will last for ever, once the war is won.

When we can sleep in our beds at night,
walk without fear, and turn on our lights.

But tonight is quiet, as the moon lights the sky,
and the stars twinkle down, could peace be nigh!

Hazel Lancaster

June - Sept - Dec 1940

June -   He was seventeen and still at school
         Life was for living and fun
         He studied hard and played all sports
         He could row, he could swim, he could run

Sept -   He was eighteen and just left school
         Hitler's war had just begun
         They gave him a uniform and tin hat
         In his hand they put a gun

Dec -   He was still eighteen and at a harder school
         He learned to fight and use that gun
         Now he lies in mud, with the friends of his youth
         His life, so brief, is done!

Peggy Love

Sonnet Blue Years

Blue tunic finally was mine to don;
I took my stance, an erk, upon the square,
But now with none to fight, as war scarce done,
It seemed that not to fly was most unfair:
Yet destined not for me propellered thrill,
For air-crew then were numbered less in flight;
I had the knowledge - thought to learn the skill
And found cadets had not a prior right:
My feet remained attached to office-ground;
My basic task - help free long-serving men
And women too, as thus I quickly found
That, to this end, my call to push a pen:
  But while demob awaited she fair-haired
  Was I myself within her wiles ensnared.

W Roy Harvey

Forties Fear

The sirens wailed at two am,
We clambered out of bed.
An air raid warning yet again;
'Downstairs!' my Mother said.

In the cellar all was still
Till guns began to boom.
Then shrapnel clattered in the yard
And flashes lit the room.

My sister smiled so bravely when
The drone of planes came near.
'Is this the end?' my brother cried;
His voice was tinged with fear.

We didn't die, but hundreds did
In London and elsewhere,
As terror hurtled from the sky
Without a thought or care.

But think before you blame those planes
Or pilots for their sin.
Mothers died and babies, too,
In Dresden and Berlin.

Leslie Scheftsik

Get Fell In

We want you for a soldier boy,
The call-up people said,
I thought *My God,* how awful,
I may even end up dead.

I was young and I was skinny,
But it didn't seem to matter.
The MO felt all round and said,
'Army food will make you fatter.'

They sent me a free warrant,
To Budbrooke, Warwickshire.
A barracks where the NCO's
Were six feet tall, and fond of beer.

With rifles weighing half a ton,
We drilled and dashed about.
'I bet old Hitler's worried now,'
The NCO's would shout.

To the rifle range we went,
And almost shot the adjutant,
Until a sergeant, quite surprised,
Found one recruit with faulty eyes.

They taught us how to read a map,
For night-time exercises,
Half our platoon were lost till noon,
The AA found the skivers.

We passed out six weeks later
Being almost on our knees.
We fought and fought, it came to naught,
We still were posted overseas.
M V Bayes

Spring 1942

As though no petal bloomed, no lark was singing,
As if the sun had set, the stars had died,
Steel-hooved satanic chargers leap the continents,
Spurning God's noon to meet their eventide.

And just as though there had not been total war,
No screaming gun-song, no Dictators' reign,
Still from the scarred, blind copse and woodland soar
The witless, joyous birds, and here
I watch green buds again.

Charles Ackerman Berry

A Fairytale from the Forties

In our teens
And somewhat sad.
No coupons,
Nothing new
To wear,
And Christmas
Nearly here.

However,
In our factory
Worked a good fairy.
Proud owner of that
Girl's best friend,
A sewing machine.

She knew a wizard.
With a stock of
Black-out stuff.
He supplied
She sewed.
Until we were
All stitched up,
In new black dresses.
From our very own
Black Market.

Leah Skinner

Sweet Sorrow

He whispers endearments in my ear,
As we meander through green leafy glade,
With sun dappled grass beneath our feet; -
Birds, sing in unison, on this God-given day!

A young soldier on leave, from a war at its height,
On leave with his young bride-to-be;
We are both so aware of a parting tonight;
And *Troopship*, taking him back o'er the sea!

So much is at stake in this war-torn world,
But for these brief moments forget, -
And savour in memory, be-jewelled river as it curls,
And sweet - scented clover, dew - wet!

So soon to part for the great unknown -
Precious hours to treasure as we talk!
We speak of a future, filled with faith, love and hope;
And other *sweet dreams* - as we walk!

We pray for the strength, to *win through* for each other;
To survive the carnage and strife;
To carry on, - to that *wonderful day*,
When together, we will start a new life!

Gertrude Parsons

55

Tribute

These prattling, empty headed girls,
When the war began.
Sacrificed their carefree life,
Worked hard as any man.
Forswore their paint and powder,
To run the factories.
They tilled the land with dirty hands,
In grubby dungarees.
And when the war was over,
And peace returned again,
They blossomed in their finery,
Like flowers after rain.

D T Baker

Lost Soul

In the forties I went to war
Called up to do my bit
Now I wonder what it was for
When I view the world as I sit.
Young lives were lost in the air, sea and land
Have we counted the cost? Can we understand
Why anyone wants to kill another
For the sake of religion and land
Why can't we respect and love our brother
Whatever his colour or creed
Why must we always hate - want revenge
Instead of helping another in need?
The forties were years of stress and fear
Bombs and fighting year after year.
I was a soldier who loved my wife
But war became a way of life
It was hard to settle when I came home
I couldn't resist the urge to roam
No more a family life for me
I had to feel that I was free
I lost my way when the war was done
I was neither husband, father or son.

Edna Wilcox

The Forties

Life in the forties was grim,
Life in the forties was fun.
The boys were in the Forces
Fighting against the Hun.

Women took the place of men
And did some pretty good work .
In the WRNS, the WAAF, the ATS,
And from factory grind didn't shirk.

Such a great feeling of belonging;
It's hard to imagine now,
But people smiled, and shared
The little their coupons would allow.

The atmosphere was wonderful;
It would have been a great life
If it weren't for the bombs and the killings,
The horrors of war, and the strife!

Mid-forties the war was over
And back to normal we came,
Grumbled about the shortages,
And everyone else was to blame.

But the prisons weren't so full,
And women could go out at night
Without fear of mugging or worse,
Though the streets still hadn't much light.

I suppose some things have improved,
But I really do long for the times
When children went to school unescorted,
With hundreds percent fewer crimes.
Helena Kerr

Lament on London Bridge

1934

On London Bridge in the Green of the year,
She stands serene and knows not fear.
Downstream - Tower Bridge agape,
Whilst a white ship slips through
To join barges and boats at Hay's wharf.
Cranes are rising and descending
With rhythm; counterpointing
The slap of tide on piles and baulking.
she is engulfed by the sound, the sun, the syncopation;
But shakes off the inclination
Not to return to occupation.

1949

On London Bridge in the Fall of the year,
She stands in sorrow, for life is drear.
Downstream Tower Bridge immobile,
A stately Pile for tourist or scholar.
Hay's wharf deserted, somnolent.
Only the memory of trampling feet
Of soldiers crossing the busy street.

Turning Citywards she sought
A once new office building, wrought
Iron gated and paved forecourt.
No trace remained - victim of a bomb.
The church where lunch-time concerts
Relieved the long day's tedium -
Gone, nothing left but shrubs and seats.
A retreat for recreation,
No charge for admission.
By memories saddened she weeps;
'Oh Lord, preserve *this* from Atomic Fission!'

May Lee

What Price War!

To those in the forties who lost the lot!
Heart-broken...yet, uncomplaining they got
On with the job, however hard to do,
Which took courage...yes, a special kind, too!

To those who for their country their lives gave;
For them no honours; just an unknown grave;
In a foreign land to forever sleep;
For them no flowers; for them no one to weep.

To those who worked on munitions; who knew
Blown to bits they could be, many were, too;
Yet...tired, nerves frayed they worked night and day...
Turned out the shells which blew Hitler away.

To those who in Civvy Street did their bit
Which went unnoticed...so what? They ne'er quit;
Kept their sense of fun when 'round them bombs fell
Which turned folk's lives into a living hell!

To those who had nightmares through what they saw
And experienced; the horrors of war
Which left them marked for life, in more ways than
One...all through the insane power-lust of man!

To those who were children when war came; who
For safety were sent away; who fret, too;
Felt homesick...ne'er showed it but within wept;
Being Brits; a stiff, tight upper lip kept.

To those who when the war came to an end...
Had to, alas, the rest of their lives spend
In hospital, wheelchairs; crippled and blind
Through vile war which shames the name of mankind.
Jackie Holroyd

Munitions

'Come-on my girl, you're needed, I'm sure you'll agree,
the war has just started, for you and for me,
We must all pull together, put our backs to the wheel,
The foe's to be beaten,' the Government feels.

Down the rows of oiled pistons, we traversed each day,
It wasn't all hardship, we always made hay,
One girl who played *hooky* to go dancing you see,
The Manager found her and said 'Follow me.'
Dressed all in her finery, she sat at the wheel,
While hot burrs flew around her, they were far from genteel.

As midnight came round, we stopped for our meal,
The workshop was quiet, *navvies alley* was still,
A screech broke the silence, 'Oh my God, I declare...
I've posted my sandwiches on the way here!
The posties face tomorrow, will be funny no doubt,
When he finds it's my dinner, that he's taken out.'

The forties were lovely, even with all the strife,
we just hoped it would make for a much better life,
But as I sit and reflect on the things of the past,
I'm sure as heck happy... we had things that did last,
They were grey days for certain, but no doubt the best,
For I wouldn't give a thank you... for all the rest.
With the time that is left, I'll make sure that I find
All the best of the future... with my past in mind.

Jenny Horrocks

A Photo Taken in 1940

Look at this girl with such abundant hair
Swept wavily back from her smooth brow,
Look at that mouth ready to laugh away woes
Those eager eyes which say *ready to go now*

Merrily, she did go into the Land Army
And worked hard with right good will
From dawn to dusk until her hands were sore
Picking potatoes - her laughter rings there still.

After the war, she returned to the city,
Though she longed for the bright skies;
She got a job typing dull business mail:
When she married Fred; her world was stews and pies.

Retired in 1993, she returned to the country,
Her hair has lost its lustre, her brow is creased,
But her eyes are still eager, her laugh is gay,
With Fred by her side, all yearning has ceased.

Mary Frances Mooney

The Auctioneer 1946

How'm I bid? Fourteen fat lambs,
the pride of Mr Carr, a man of substance and of sense,
as all good farmers are!
Who'll start me off? Now come along,
it's great to be alive on such a market day as this.
A start at forty-five? Fifty, fifty, fifty five?
Who'll sixty boldly say?
Come! Fine fat lambs of Romney Marsh
are worth much more today.
I sold such lambs at Biddenden
for three and eighty bob.
Sam, give those lambs a stir about.
They think we're here to rob!
Ah! Thank you sir. I take the bid at sixty.
Sixty one? Who pulls my leg?
I'll call it four, now seven from Mr Munn.
Sixty seven? The price is cheap.
Who'll buy the lot for eight?
They tell me ol' John Winter's here.
He's bidding pretty late.
Eight now it is. Eight. Any more? I say at eight.
Do I hear nine from Mr Walter Gore?
Nine then it is. It goes at nine.
You'll lose them, Mr Fenn.
Going, going at sixty nine.
Gone. Gore of Wissenden.
Next lot.

George Pearson

Please don't Trample on my Cowslip!

Long years ago when we were only children
And life was simple, *doing as you're told,*
We set off to the meadows with a basket
To plunder heads of gleaming cowslip gold.

There were so many then, a scented carpet
Of golden bells alive with honeybees.
The world was dewy-fresh and unpolluted.
No tractors, just the murmuring hedgerow trees.

In childhood days the sun seemed always shining.
In memory, the Spring was always fine.
Our mothers took the fragrant heaps of flowers
And gradually turned them into wine.

Last year, a tiny packet labelled *cowslip*
Was opened, sown, and tended with great care.
Just three plants grew, and this year one had flowers.
The garden border now boasts something rare!

Audrey Forbes-Handley

We Regret

Above the snarling, pitiless roar,
Of the grinding, screeching machines of war,
The silence of grief is felt once more.
Oh God. . . when will man ever learn?
(Another loved one will never return).
She carries on. . . (life must go on).
We'll meet again,. . . (she joins in song).
Hiding away. . . when shadows creep,
To lick her wounds alone. . . and weep.
Then, thro' the mists of anguished, turbulent sleep,
She saw him rise from an angry deep.
His smile. . . so sad. . . *Be brave my love. . . my dearest one,*
He needs you now, our little son.
She woke. . . to find the vision gone.
It's just a dream,. . . she knew. . . and yet,
The hope that eased her aching heart. . .
The first since the telegram,
We Regret.

M Maidment

65

Take Off

Thundering down the runway
Eyes bright - one red - one green,
Wings bristling, guns at the ready
Like dragons in old tales
Seeking their prey.
We watched in the gathering gloom,
At steady intervals they rose
Soaring into the darkening sky.
Our hearts went with them -
We prayed for their safe return,
Never thinking about the recipients
Of the deadly pay load.
Then in the cold grey dawn
We watched again, counting them back
Hope and dread clutching at our hearts.

Ivy Allpress

Living in the Forties

I remember, I remember,
The planes, the bombs, the cries,
As fire and death rained down on earth
From planes up there in the skies.

I remember, I remember,
The crosses on the graves,
As kith and kin were snatched from life -
And by death were made slaves.

I remember, I remember,
The men who gave their lives
From both world wars - their names recall -
Their children, families, wives.

Yes - memory 'tis a blessed gift
In retrospect to see
The past and all that's taken place
If better men we be!

If looking back, we lessons learn -
To build a future sure -
When planes and bombs and people's cries
Once heard - will be no more.

However, memory's not enough
To guarantee such peace.
The government of God we need
If man's wars are to cease.

Jeanne Boffey

The Forties

Come back in time with me
When beer was fourpence and sixpence a pint
Sweets and clothes were on ration
And policemen were always in sight

No cars crowded our streets
Not many buses came by
Journey's were mostly by bike
And only the birds did fly

Work was for everyone
Nobody had to slack
And nobody had to lock up a bike
It would be there when you came back

One could leave doors unlocked
Nobody would have entered
Burglary was hardly a done thing
And mugging was not invented

Women were quite safe
They would not be harried
Armed robbery was not a done thing
As guns were not carried

This is life in the forties I remember
Forties of war and peace
Now we have murder, rape, and corruption
When will it all cease

A Saunders

A Memory of the Roaring Forties

My lover sails the ocean,
He has sailed the seven seas,
And with a rocking motion
He is walking out with me.
The girls are always staring,
I don't know why they do?
It may be what I'm wearing
For, my boy in navy blue.

A sailor's girl is jolly,
To put up with what they do?
He sometimes, calls me Dolly,
When my name is Lindy Lou.
The girls are always talking,
I don't know why they do?
It may be that I'm walking
With, romance, wrapped up in blue.

And when I've hitched that sailor,
With a bowline and a ring.
He'll find I'll be his jailor,
Like a vine, I'll ever cling.
The girls are always wrangling,
I don't know why they do?
It may be that I'm angling,
For, my boy in navy blue.
Oh! I love that sailor guy,
Tho' he's only five feet high.
With a smile that's gay and free,
He is walking out, with me!

Cyril Carter

69

Gaslight

It was only a small group of people near
the lamp-post that misty night,
not more than ten or perhaps eleven at the most.
Being nine years old I didn't really know
why Dad and me were there at all.
Nobody seemed to have much to say, as though,
in a way, it would have broken a spell.
I could tell Dad didn't want to leave,
just wanted to stand there and share the
splutter of gaslight after years of
stumbling around in the dark. Dad, having been
in the ARP always said that the spark
from a lighted match could be seen by
enemy bombers four miles up.

But the lamp showed a new beginning
symbolic of our winning.
My thanks to the few
who pulled us all through
alive
in '45.

Shirley F Winskill

Hello and Goodbye

An army convoy thunders down Market Street
On its way to a Staging Camp
Hooray! There'll be plenty of partners for Saturday's hop
No more wallflowers - they'll be a thing of the past
A surplus of men at last.

No stockings in the shops so apply gravy browning
Sugar and water solution to set the curls
And maybe borrow Auntie's pearls
Disused velvet curtains can be cut up for a dress
And very high heeled shoes, no less.

An army quartet provided the band
Excellent musicians - give them a big hand
First half is lively to get all on the floor
Soldier's preferring to drink beer
Are let out of the door.

After the interval smoochy music, the lights turned low
Couples glide, bodies pressed close to each other
All too soon - the Last Waltz - saxophone sobbing.

Out into the blackout, arms linked, a brisk trot home
He musn't be late back or he'll end up in the Guardroom!

Doorstep kisses - their growing intensity halted
By Dad's special cough as he plans to put the cat out.

Break-away! Fingers entwine then trail apart

I'll think of you darling while I'm overseas
Promise not to forget me - promise, please.

I promise sure as the stars above
Go now. Goodbye my love.

Doreen Duce

Secret Wedding

Things were very different then, in nineteen forty seven
That was the year when we got wed, and thought we were in Heaven!
Wedding rings were ten pounds each, in twenty two carat gold, but
second-hand
And fairly rare, at the jeweller's we're told.
As a hopeful bride I wanted a ring that belonged to me alone
So chose a nine carat carefully carved with diamond shapes - nice tone!
At 9am we plied our troth, with only two to witness
At Registrar's Office - we wanted no fuss or arguments to fitness!
I'd saved up my coupons, for a brand new suit, *utility* my dear,
But the blue silk blouse, was a luxury I had to have, 'twas clear!
No bouquet just a moss-rose spray, and we meant our vows forever,
Though not in church, they meant the same, and still do, now and ever.
Money was scarce and rations were few, a friend made the cake and rum in
it too!
Tiny boxes to send to relations, we'd hoped to placate for not *having a do*
It wasn't successful, they never forgave us -
Let this be a lesson to you!

Kate Fell

August 1939

Down the Back Dykes, nothing moves,
No hurrying feet or clopping hooves;
The street lies quiet in golden haze,
All doors are closed to sunlight's rays.
Auld Aggie Daw's bright bobbing smile
Has left her doorstep for a while;
The Knowe is empty, still and bare,
No Tam or Jim or Davy there.
In Johnston Square, the sunshine plays
On balconies and staircase ways;
Its patterns weave o'er rail and mat
And warms a fat old slumbering cat.
No *penter's whistle* sharp and shrill,
Is winged across from Joe to Bill.
No balls are stotted on the wall,
No noisy children's prattling call.
The silence hangs like heavy hand
As if a voice had stilled the land;
But, all is well, this bright fine day,
It's three o'clock, down East Wemyss way.

Janet Brown

Life in the Forties

War was declared, I was terrified.
The wireless told us this news.
Gas masks issued frightened me. I cried.

Blackout curtains were hung, this was the law.
Sticky brown paper criss crossed our windows.
One pushed through thick blankets to get in the door.

Ration books, sugar coupons, life's pattern for the future
Spuds and cabbages replaced flowers in the front garden.
A bed or a table? - Dockets for utility furniture.

Dried egg, spam and whale meat.
Wedding cakes a large cardboard fraud, a little sponge inside!
When at last we could queue for a banana, what a treat.

Our lovely sandy beaches were a non zone.
Great metal spikes all across the water line.
This to keep the Germans away, we did not moan.

School friends were soon in uniform,
Fighting, working for our country.
Call ups were soon the norm.

Sadly, many did not come back.
We *all* mourned such people.
Soldier, sailor, airman, John or Jack.

Many a night, and day, in our shelters we sat.
(We soon learned the sounds of enemy planes and buzz bombs)
Grandma, baby, the dog *and* the cat!

We all worked together, our aim was for peace
Sharing, caring, laughing, crying.
Nothing would stop us, until hostilities cease.

Peggy Buckett

The Spoils of War

We didn't know when the war was won
We'd be cold and hungry for years to come.

Family planning was not in vogue
We loved having our husbands at home.

We were rather like Mary the mother of God
Our babies were born unexpectedly.

The snow fell thick when we went into labour
Christmas loomed with no turkey to cook.

Even potatoes were rationed and bread
Things got worse as our babies were weaned.

How did we manage? It's easy to answer
We were just glad to be alive and kicking.

We hadn't lost our hope for the future
We knew things could only get better.

Fools? Yes; but we had such potential
We worked hard for the new generation.

Was it worth it? Don't make me sick!
Meet my grandsons Elvis and Mick.

Gladys Birmingham

I Was a WAAF

In forty one, I went to war. My friend came too, (the one next door).
We'd been good mates since we were five, and thought it great to be alive,
At infant school we both were shy, the boys had always made us cry.
But by the time that we were eight, they'd swing us on the garden gate.
Then young misses aged thirteen, young ladies when we reached nineteen.
The years till then had been so kind, how could we have been so blind,
Wrapped up in our own sweet life, not to see the clouds of strife
Banking up there in the west, we were not a bit depressed,
For war was never going to be; so my friend had said to me.
We were both so very wrong for it wasn't all that long,
By the close of year, September; came the day we would remember,
The words were grave, the voice so sad, *we are at war* oh God, that's bad!
But in our hearts a little song, *never mind, it won't last long!*
Once again we thought we knew, (perhaps the same thought came to you!)
Two years later, forty-one, my life in civvy street was done.
I proudly wore the blue of the WAAF, so did my pal who's name was
Daph;
We learned to drive and passed together, out in every sort of weather.
But it was great we loved it all, the different jobs, it didn't pall.
We drove tractors, bombs on trailers, coaches, staff cars, had no failures.
For every job just seemed the same, to use it was a great big game.
We had to do all that we could, to get us all out of the wood.
And we never felt too down, off duty *really went to town,*
To help us to forget our sorrow that we might not have tomorrow.
This was up to all the gods, but we had some very good odds,
For we were never in the *line,* but didn't mind that, that was fine,
We did our duty come what may, I'll always remember to this day,
Those years together in the WAAF, now sixty-seven, me and old Daph!

Doris J Baldwin

78

Those Dancing Years

Those were the days a long time ago
When dancing people, faces all aglow
The dance hall was crowded all through the night
Dancing feet, some clumsy some very light
A long walk to the dance hall we had
Even when the weather was very bad
The music was played by a great band
One could say it was the best in the land
The dancers were in uniform, the civvies only a few
There was airmen, soldiers, and boys in blue
A dance hall was the only place we went
Where we lived there was very little entertainment
We were all happy in those years
Although people shed a lot of tears
The dances kept one going you know
This was in wartime a long time ago.

Mary Butters

More Than a Matter of Life and Death

One Saturday in Sixty Six,
we all sat down in a darkened room,
the fate of the nation was at stake,
clouds of contention began to loom.
The country wide was on alert,
dire threats to our brave young men,
the dreaded Hun was at the door.
Was it thirty nine all over again?
As the battle unfolded before our eyes,
Auntie Kit nearly had a heart attack,
my dear old Mum could hardly watch,
our defiant defence must not crack.
The conflict raged both long and hard
with many a mighty challenge made,
no quarter given and none was sought,
shot after shot in a fusillade.
My wife, ashen faced, fled the stressful scene,
and I cowered, flinching, in my chair,
hostilities reaching the closing call,
it was all too much for us to bear.
As we fearfully awaited the final blow,
our strength and resolve almost gave up,
then the merciful arbiter brought the fight to an end,
England had, at last, won football's World Cup!

Michael Webb

A Night in the Forties

The ballroom door burst open
We were invaded by The Yanks
The chewing gum
The Hi Babe
The Do You Wanna Dance
Ration books forgotten
Also Hitler and his gang
This was one night to remember
Listening to Glen Miller and his band
We would face the sirens warning
And the horrors it would bring
Roll Out the Barrel
Is the song that we would sing
Each decade leaves its memories
Some pass - some linger on
The forties were special years
They united everyone.

Monica Drury

A Day in the Life of a Landgirl

Forget all your dresses and lovely silk hose;
Put on breeches and wellies instead,
For you're going to do the work of a man;
Stick your *pork-pie* hat on your head.

Put your nose round the door, there's a white frost outside,
And there's kale in the fields to be cut.
It's no use complaining so brace yourself up
And harness the horse to the putt.

Then when that's done and it's spread in the field,
The cows will be out there to eat;
So you can go in and muck out the stall,
Scrub the floor, and make it all neat.

Next, William the Bull will be waiting for you.
Take care in case he *sees red.*
Clean him out quick - don't touch his hind legs -
Good thing there's two doors in his shed!

The wee orphan lambs must be bottle-fed;
The calves must be given their hay;
There are eggs to collect, and the time's getting late.
Oh, for more hours in a day!

With the rain on your face, and the wind in your hair,
And an overcoat weighing a ton,
With a back fit to break, and two rough, blistered hands,
The life of a landgirl is fun!

Irene Attwell

Hour Glass

Before that day
The war evaded my attention.
Glass rings from crashing planes,
On main roads with roller skates,
Sun on my face and climbing trees,
Hands stretched for army sweets,
Dried out eggs and water glass.
Before that day,
Passing seven, D Day at the sea,
Wet hair and sandy cousins,
Bare legs chill and crabs in pools,
Salt on my face, and seaweed popping
Under gritty feet, sea smell,
Winkles, shrimps and waving grass.
Before that day,
A telegram from another beach:
Leaden sand, and brazen shells.
My uncle, less than twenty.
Salt on my face. The violinist,
Dead earth on silent hands.
Small, hard waste as battles pass.
Before that day,
I had not known that grown ups wept.
Grief percolated childhood.
Fear drifted in the cracks,
Sun on my face, wet my mother's tears.
An absolute in happiness,
Being seven. But then, alas,
Before that day.

Sue Cooper

83

Willie's Dilemma

Willie was a plumber, fully qualified was he,
Bilingual, as those in that trade are said to be.
With pipes, joints, stop-cocks, washers or a U-bend,
Any plumbing calamity he could renew or mend.
If a job was difficult and problems then arose,
He often used foul *Lingo* in unprintable prose.

On shipping in the Docks, was his working domain,
In wartime, *Reserved*, so a civilian had to remain.
The work was hard, hours long and often quite erratic.
Up funnels, masts, below decks, in tanks, he was never static.
Under all conditions, - in raids, and any weather hot or cold,
Datelines to be met, needed a worker, fit and bold.

The tough clothes worn, seldom stood the strain,
Often received rips, tears and many a nasty stain.
Clothes rationing drove Willie's wife, almost to despair,
Struggling with *Make Do and Mend*, for every new repair.
The items to be mended most, that never stood the test,
Were armpit holes, in Willie's short-sleeved woollen vests.

To ensure her spouse against the cold would be protected,
Willie's wife, for him, long-legged woolly pants selected.
Though grateful for her kindness, he refused to co-operate.
Stated, in thick clothes, his job was difficult to operate,
Climbing high up masts and ladders, exercising care,
Needing to move freely, those *Long Johns* he would not wear.

One day, having torn vest sleeves to renew,
Willie's wife knew exactly what she had to do.
The legs from those *Long Johns*, made a neat repair,
And Hubby then had short-legged pants to spare.
Laughingly she pondered, as to work he went,
With arms in the legs of his pants, did he set a precedent?
Ethel L Thake

84

Living in the 40's

Wartime came to the milltowns.
Gone the weavers *boom*.
Anti-aircraft batteries, everywhere.
Taking over from the loom.
Soldiers, came to the milltowns.
Pubs were full all day.
Judy, started drinking.
(There was the *hell to pay*)
Schoolgirls grew up faster.
Hanging round army camps.
Husbands, had gone off to war.
(Some houses, had red lamps!)
Blackmarket spivs were active.
Selling *dodgy* goods.
Where they came from, no one knew.
Or whether they were *duds!*
Local lads, were pushed aside.
Soldiers, were more exciting.
Willing girls, were left behind.
To do their own *nail biting*.
Evacuees, then, did arrive.
With families, taken in.
Squashed in little bedrooms.
No room to put a pin.
So when the war was over.
And peace reigned over all.
We welcomed home our loved ones.
Who had answered to the call.

Joy Phillips

Love in Nineteen Forty-One

It is always cold the evenings we spend
In this shadowy brown room,
Inside the tiny wartime cafe.
We close the curtained door quickly, protectively.
Stray beams should not filter the stern outside dark.
The brave glow from shaded lamps
Draws us to the red checked tables.
The dark-haired girl, familiar in little-girl flat
Ankle strapped shoes, smiles a welcome, warming us.
'Quiet tonight. No air-raid yet.' Maybe recalling
A recent landmine explosion, incredibly survived.
We study the sparse menu. Wryly choosing
Beans on toast, we hold our breath, watching her -
(Will she captivate us again, and offer poached eggs?)
Ah well. We order - two coffees please. And sigh.

Alone, we touch and whisper 'I love you.'
Lighting cigarettes, we watch the smoke
Weaving up and into, dimmed, ghostly corners.
The siren goes. We stay, enfolded in our microcosm.
Others assail shelters, cloistered underground.
            'What shall we wish for?' he asks
His dear eyes strained.
'Lighted streets, butter, cream.
A floaty wedding dress. A rosy day.
A room, our own, our very own, to share.'
            'And then?'
I gaze into the kaleidoscopic landscape, far off
In a shifting world.
Then whisper 'I don't know. I can't tell.
Only peace. Just peace. Only that.'

Jessica Lack

The Raw Recruit

Up like the lark he takes his mark
Out on the square when it is quite dark.
The morning cold chills to the bone
As the raw recruit longs to be at home.

Forwards and backwards he turns about,
To right to left at the sergeant's shout.
In heavy boots his festering feet
Scream for release from the awful heat.

As days speed past his steps get light
Trained like this he is fit to fight.
Like any soldier in the line,
He is smart and tough to rise and shine.

Ready now for the Hitler foe
Across the seas where he did go
The raw recruit goes off to bring
Peace that he and others were to win.

Tom Buchanan

Our Back Street Shop

Our Corner Shop was a real gem,
A pity there are not more of them,
For on their wooden shelves stacked high,
Were many things that pleased the eye.

For whiter wash, a penny Dolly Blue,
For family wash, a penny Carbosil too,
Wooden clothes pegs for the line,
Mother praying it would be fine.

A penny black-lead for the grate,
A job that Mother used to hate,
Bundled sticks in strong black wire,
Thin steel draw plates for the fire.

Brushes, *nit* combs, for the child's head,
Queer shaped brushes to apply black-lead,
Brasso, for knobs on doors or bed,
Needles, thimbles and black thread.

Two ounce of sugar, or of tea,
And perhaps an egg for your tea,
Cheese in muslin tightly wrapped,
And bacon that was not pre-packed.

A half-penny bag of sherbet, and a liquorice stick,
All the kids would want a lick,
Aniseed balls, and bubble gum,
Or a strip of chewing gum.

You could call in every day,
Then settle up on Dad's pay-day,
'Twas what you would call a General Store,
But alas! It's not there anymore.
George Porter

On the Home Front

The announcement came steady and clear
With the dreaded words, *we are at war*. . .
I had looked at the wireless disbelieving,
The words still echoed from the year before.

As the blackout came into being
No splinter of light must be seen.
Identity cards for all to carry.
The years that followed were long and lean.

Food was sparse upon the ground
So to every person a *Ration Book*
Dividing and planning in advance
Was a challenge for me, the cook.

We worked the fields with horses
Setting cabbages and potatoes,
Back-breaking work from dawn to dusk,
Planting them in long straight rows.

Gas masks were the order of the day
And special cribs for the newborn,
Even when the warning sirens sounded
In the middle of the night or crack of dawn.

'Planes droning, bombs dropping,
People running, houses falling.
Then, deathly silence reigning.
Last voices whimpering and calling.

D-Day brought singing and dancing,
Rejoicing and rebuilding a nation.
More food, more clothes, more freedom.
A country worthy for the next generation.
Daisy Williamson

Living in the Forties

From teenager to wife and mother - surely there could be no other
Span of years with so much change, as within the Forties range!
Battle of Britain in our sky - Dunkirk miracle, to belie
Hitler's claim to conquer all - Churchill's mighty rallying call.
Bombing raids both night and day - trains and buses find their way
Among the debris - so we work - this is a duty we'll not shirk.
The RAF calls for our men - for Douglas, Sid and Freddie, then
The latter one abroad must go - how thankful then we did not know
It would be three point five years ere, his company again we'd share.
Conscripted into ATS - what a change, not without stress.
Parted from my family, a communal life is now for me.
With marching, training, discipline, to work with Radar is the thing.
On camp-sites, muddy, lonely too, our *rocket missiles* then were new!
Days off were spent in local town - one shop for fish and chips renown.
The films shown at the cinema took us away to places far.
Or else along the cliff we'd roam - in solitude to think of home.
From Wales to Yorkshire by the sea - perhaps an Officer's life for me?
Three months spent at Windsor *school* - I have first *pip*, so I'm no fool!
Signed up for year, before demob, in Admin now I do my job.
The war is over - church bells ring, and lights switch on and we can sing
For joy, with loved ones back with us; of course for them we'll make a
                                                                    fuss.

Our uniforms we've put away, we're planning now for wedding day.
'Spite shortages with rationing, the family help with everything.
To Freddie I become a wife - together we will share new life;
And make one too, in Forty-nine, when birth of daughter is the sign
That life goes on, though history's made, by changing world in one decade.

Grace Smith

90

The War Nurseries

In the Summer of '43.
All gathered in the nursery.
The siren goes, no time to waste,
Off to the shelter with great haste.

Singing nursery rhymes to pass the time,
All are seated in a line.
Humpty Dumpty and Little Boy Blue,
Little Bo Peep and Jack and Jill.

Then from the back, a request from Sandra,
'Can we sing Away in a Manger?'
Their voices rang out on that Summer's day,
And chased the German planes away.

For no sooner had we finished the song,
Than the all clear sounded and before very long.
We were able to finish the day,
Back in the nursery in the normal way.

They've had their dinner and their daily nap,
A favourite story and a game of catch.
Now all dressed up in their going home clothes,
To wait for Mum when the factories close.

Ida Cunningham

Meadow Sweet

It was the Summer of nineteen forty-one,
Almost two years since the war had begun -
Sam came home whenever he got leave,
Each visit like a small reprieve. . .
And we wandered in the nearby fields,
Enjoying the precious hours of our time together. . .
How soon we would be parted . . . maybe for ever -
Sam told me about the flowers of the field,
He knew most of them by name . . .
Tansy and Coltsfoot, Hawkweed and Grounsel,
The tall yellow Ragwort, and the shy Scarlet Pimpernel -
And the marshmallow by the stream.
Many times I looked at them in later years
Through a veil of tears . . .
Imagining what might have been -
'And here, my darling, is Meadow-sweet,
Queen of the Meadows, they say . . . the old folks made a tea
With this, to chase sickness away.'
I remember that Summer so clearly, the year Sam's son was born,
When we walked in green fields of old England,
And gazed on the ripening corn -
But I turn to the Queen of the Meadows with special love
In my heart, thinking of us . . . and all lovers
Who that Summer must part - Meadow-sweet smelling of honey,
Became Bitter-sweet in the end, as the boys all clad in
Their Battledress marched away to fight and defend -
I never saw my love again, couldn't believe in a tender refrain
But the flowers of the meadows . . .
They always bloom again.

Noni Fanger

The Days of the Forties

The days of the forties are still fresh in my mind,
A war had begun that would affect all mankind,
Food rationing had started, people queued up for bread,
Air raid warnings, kept us from sleeping in bed.

Beaten in Europe our soldiers came home,
But everyone was determined to fight on alone,
Women went to factories, and worked the machines,
With turban shaped headscarves, in trousers and jeans.

A home guard was formed, by men from the Great War,
Confident they could beat the Germans once more,
Each day on parades or as sentries they stood,
With imitation rifles made out of wood.

The forties were critical, but no one despaired
With Winston Churchill, the man at the head,
His speeches instilled the will to win,
As the battle of Britain was about to begin.

Our Merchant Navy defied the U boats,
Brought home, materials, and food for us folks,
The battle of Britain was fought and won,
Bravely our Airforce had beaten the Hun.

After victory with Montgomery at Alemein,
Slowly we made progress, began to gain,
All the territory that was previously lost,
Italy surrendered at the Germans' cost.

The invasion of Europe, via the Normandy route,
Had the enemy on the run, with the Allies in pursuit,
A combined effort by forces, from the free world,
With Russians in Berlin, the war came to an end.
A Saunders

Ode to my Dear Old Mum

At the local laundry my Mum was a scrubber
Washing clothes with a rubber dubber
It was hard work for my dear old Mum
To quench her thirst she chewed some gum.

I saw a bubble on your lips the foreman said
My dear old Mum just looked then shook her head
The foreman got cross then he spoke
You've got the sack for eating soap.

Us seven kids she had to feed
Busy looking after all our needs
Some soup from her stays she made
It tasted of old cotton, yellow with age.

We were so hungry we didn't even talk
Just kept eating the soup with only a fork
Some days a candle was lit, then with a shout
Here's light refreshment, have a good blow out.

Life was hard at our poor home
Our Italian Dad had buzzed off to Rome
My Mum then had a lodger, or so she said
Space was short so they shared one bed.

One day she smiled and said, now don't be mad
Now listen you kids, you've got a new Dad
He had a good job with lots of money
Now we ate our bread with jam and honey.

Life was good, he was here to stay
Then he buzzed off the other day
Poor Mum's back scrubbing, it ain't no joke
Working hard and again eating soap.
P Pugh

Home Sweet Home

Oh, what a lovely place is home sweet home
It is where you are treated best
Especially if you have loved ones
That share your troubles, and your fears
But there comes a day, when one has to leave
And you are left alone, and feel so lost
That's when you have to count the cost
You question, can you ever be happy again
You miss doing the washing for them
And cooking their meals, and so many things
You are always being reminded
When you see the empty chair.
But most of all, is the loved one's voice
That you will never hear again
And the presence that you will never see
But try and not get too despondent
There are millions like you and me
I have my own little private memories
No one can enter there
So hold on to your dreams, and memories
And we will get there never fear.

M A Topping

95

Yesteryear

When children walked to school and back, the horse was transport
means.
The village folk knew one and they all joined in country scenes.
When local bobby earned respect, and used to live next door.
For this was *Merrie England* as in the days of yore.

When church festivals were held with choirs both old and young.
The songs of praise and anthems with joyful hearts were sung.
When all things centred round the church's ever open door.
For this was *Merrie England* as in the days of yore.

When Easter bells rang cross the air to tell the wondrous news.
And children walked to Sunday school, new dresses and new shoes.
The chocolate eggs were something fine, and made to last full score.
For this was *Merrie England* as in the days of yore.

When fields were ploughed with horses very smart and powerful strong.
Waggoners walked behind the team, and days were hard and long.
And both were glad at eventide to see the stable door.
For this was *Merrie England* as in the days of yore.

When King and Country meant a lot, to wave the flag was fine.
And people over all the world were proud to say that's mine.
And *Empire Day* a holiday round Britain's famous shore.
For this was *Merrie England* as in the days of yore.

When morris dancers did perform upon the village green.
And people came from far and wide it was a rural scene.
Then men and maids did dance and sing to music of folklore.
For this was *Merrie England* as in the days of yore.

William Arthur Littleford

Living in the Forties

Hurry hurry, dusk is falling
Soon the hell of night will start,
Death, destruction, so appalling
We all have to play our part.
Check the blackout, douse that light,
The enemy could be overhead,
A canopy of black, our night
As like moles we grope for bed
Down the shelter, or the dug-out
Where else safely could we go
From droning planes with deadly fall-out
Say goodbye to friends we know.
Shattered buildings, fireman's hoses
People dazed wander around,
Trains have stopped, and one supposes
Something's hit the underground,
Years roll by, our hearts are strong
When will all this mayhem cease
We have dropped the atom bomb
Please dear Lord let there be peace.

Marie Wood

The Nineteen Forties

The war sticks in my memory
which I recall so vividly
bombs falling round us everywhere
as we ran to the shelter or under a stair
to hide our fear we would sing some songs
or play games to help pass hours so long
sirens would sound a loud all clear
then you would check on folks that you held dear
some of these days proved to be sad
when news of friends turned out to be bad
yet life carried on with sheer determination
undaunted and brave was this generation
the people worked hard and helped one another
hosts of them lost husbands, sons or a brother
when war was over rations were few
for all your food items you always had to queue
we had lots of compensations from things of pleasure
dance halls and music we can still treasure
the films of the forties and their wonderful stars
who will live on forever in our hearts
the Beano the Dandy with old Desperate Dan
were a regular feature for a comic fan
Dick Barton on Radio and all his escapades
a serial on weekdays that was all the rage
you bathed by the fire in a big tin bath
and slept in rough blankets that made you want to scratch
utility furniture and outside loos
newspaper hung in there not fancy tissues
yet we were happy as we rebuilt our lives
living in the forties I can talk about with pride.

Patricia Barr

Anthology of the Forties

Pull over the blackout, don't show the faintest glimmer,
Overhead the enemy will see that light, waiting for a chance,
To zimmer down on target, to drop a hail of horror,
For some it spells out *finish* for them there's no tomorrow

But we will crawl out of the shambles, our spirits ever rising,
Into the munitions shed, it's our lives for which we're striving
There's *music while you work* in the middle of the morn',
Voices raise above the din, to quench the machinery's storm,

We walk out in the blackout, torches pointing low
We do not have to worry, that the muggers are in tow,
Our weekly dose of cinema - ninepence to get in,
Is to us a highlight. The most romantic fling.

Our sweetie rations finished. What else then can we chew?
While we wait for Douglas Fairbanks, and his very Motley Crew.
Then there's *Pathetone News*, oh. Not another liner sunk? Lost.
What a waste of precious lives, what a fantastic cost.

When we win this war and say, it must not happen again.
The scourge breaks out afresh, another country, just the same,
When will we cry for wisdom, to see the other point of view
Sit around the council table, and wait to see what others do?

Can we not learn from all the sacrifice and pain?
That all our brave endeavour, was reality not in vain,
Let's look to the young one's future, with very thankful hearts
Pray, that they will know true peace and joy, and never have to part.

F E Mullis

The Roaring Forties

Talking of the *Roaring Forties*
Almost seems like *Tales of Yore*,
The way we lived, even with restrictions galore.
As years passed by; and Peace came to our Nation,
Bringing joy, and so much adulation,
We remember those, who made such sacrifice,
To win that Peace, and save our lives.

The days and ways of freedom had to be learned;
Starting afresh to enjoy all we had earned.
The family life, and ability to travel;
To pick up the Past - let our Spirits' unravel.
We set forth with hope, in so many Spheres,
To look forward, encourage the next generation!
Having freedom to develop in each situation.

The end of rationing, and ability to buy;
To *deck* ourselves - to travel, and to fly;
Released from the tensions, be able to plan,
New auras to await us - new horizons to scan.
The late years of the Forties spelt hard work, but Peace,
We nurtured our children - watching them grow;
Enjoying new pleasures - they did not even know.

With all the stresses of rehabilitation,
All the advances of Science, and Education,
Over the Decades; that have come and gone;
The speed of Life, drives on the mighty throng.
The Foundations of *the Forties* that were truly made,
May they not be forgotten, or thoughtlessly mislaid.
Looking backward yes, but ever forward, to the present Generation.

Kay Fleming

Arnhem

Lots of cowboys bit the dust
And many an Injun too;
All upon that fated day
On the Bridge
At Arnhem.

Some died in bunches
Some alone;
This one was Jewish
That one a Pole;
Another simply says *unknown*.
All on one day
At Arnhem.

Now they're planted
True Dutch style.
Like a field of white tulips
Near the Bridge
At Arnhem.

David Madeira-Cole

Daylight Raid 1940

Here, in the basement shelter
Of a large department store
We sit waiting the loud *all clear*
While death rains down from the skies.
Some chat and laugh, some read, some knit,
And some are silently withdrawn,
Now, standing perchance on Death's keen edge
What passes through my mind?
A numbed acceptance of my fate
Until the child beside me
Sobs in her mother's arms.
Then anger fills my heart
That this dear three-year old
Might die before she's lived.
Oh such a rare September day
Of soft blue sky and gentle sun
She should not die.

Barbara E Morgan

Passion for Living 1940

Obscured as sunlight through a mist of rain,
Thought-treasured as a moment free from pain,
Half-only understood, a thing apart,
This was our way of life, the beating of our heart.
Yet fire burns in each one, so fierce a fire
One spark ignites a forest of desire
To give, to get, to seek, to find, to do,
To love, to laugh - to live - a full life through.

Then where-from comes the power that says that we
Should be prepared to perish, being free?
What freedom can be suffered in the grave? -
Well, those that live can say that we were brave! -
But we are here and now, and we will *be*.

Though even as we rail we know there can
Be no respite for us nor anyone
Until the light of freedom has prevailed,
Whatever cost to us may be entailed.

Thus dew damp to the fire of our just grief
Comes blessedness, cool beauty, sweet relief,
That tempers our soul's madness with its gifts
And into realms of greatness mere men lifts.
Would that we, weak or worldly, use both right
And greet with gladness our one chance to fight
To make the most of living while we can -
This is the breathing right of every man.

Doris Wilkinson

Morning on the Seine: Near Giverny by Monet

Monet's painting is full of light,
Sunrise in pearl colours,
Pinks, greens and blues,
In translucent harmony.
Reflections in the water
Double our comprehension,
Leading us into another world,
Where beauty defeats materialism.

A terrible pillar of light struck Hiroshima.
Children going to school were mutilated.
Their mothers were destroyed,
Waving goodbye at the window.
Distraught fathers
Found only small pieces of clothing,
To remind them of their children.
Some were burnt alive; some survived
Only to die a slow death
Through radiation sickness.
Devastation flattened their houses,
Leaving bare trees
With not a single leaf.

Nowadays the survivors
Can visit the Hiroshima's Museum of Art
And view Monet's painting,
Unimpaired by terror.

Hilary Edwards